Reflections

Poems

Chris M L Burleigh

Reflections

Poems

Chris M L Burleigh

This paperback edition First Published in Great Britain in 2025 by Beercott Books.

Text © Chris M L Burleigh 2024
Design & layout © Beercott Books 2025
Cover images © Chris M L Burleigh 2024

ISBN 978-1-9191834-0-4

Chris M L Burleigh has asserted his moral rights to be identified as the author of this book according to the Copyright, Designs & Patents act 1988.

All rights reserved. No part of the publication may be reproduced, stored in a retrieval system, or transmitted in any form or by any means, electronic, mechanical, photocopying, recording or otherwise, without written prior permission of the publishers and copyright holders.

This is a work of fiction. Names, characters, businesses, places, events and incidents are either the products of the author's imagination or used in a fictitious manner. Any resemblance to actual persons, living or dead, or actual events is purely coincidental.

A catalogue record of this book is available from the British Library.

Beercott Books
www.beercottbooks.co.uk

For Margaret

Contents

Life

Making Sense	3
Spring	4
Miracles	6
The Dry Summer	7
The coming of the Magi	8
Walking a Familiar Loop	9
The Sense of an Ending	10
Frost	11
Mesmerised	12
Tenses	13
No Time Like the Present	14
Life	15
Heady Days	16
Holiday	17
The Price of Principle	18
Seeing is Believing	19
Sunsets	20
Easter	22
It's Freezing	23
Yoga Retreat	23
A Life	24
No More to Sleep	26
Stained Glass	27
Solitary Existence	28
Easy Life	28
Flames	29
Hindsight	30
Sea and Shore	31
Weather Front	32
Judge Not	32
Parting	33
The Season of Goodwill is Over	34
Uninvited Guests	35
Meaningful Existence	36
The Nature of Power	37
The Sound of Silence	38
Patter	39
Transformative AI	40
Seaside	41
Being One's Self	42
The Countryman	43
Can't Afford It!	44
Sound Bites	44
Counting	45

Love

Anniversary	49
A Couple's Couplet	49
Gold'n	50
The Last Days	52
Looking Back	53

Laughter

Red or White	57
Cheers!	57
Connoisseur	58
A Poet's Life	58
Epitaph	59
Some Hope	59
Humans	60
Touch and Go	60
No-Mow May	61
Slow Down!	61
No Place, Being There	62
A Word to the Wise	62
Judge Not	63
My TBR List	63
The End of the Affair	64
A Calling	64
Donkey	65
Third Law of Diametrics	65
Like, You Mean It	66
Flat Earthers	66
Ageing	67
Reflection	67
Domestic Chores, Domestics Bores	68
Country Walk	68
Summer Drinks	69
Summer Nights	69

i

De facto Descartes	70
Opinionated Descartes	70
Techie	71
An Apple for Eve	71
Confused	72
Baldness	72
The Price of Fame/Unsung Heroes	73
Civic Pride	73
In Mitigation	74
Nirvana	74
No Fun	75
Sun Flour	75
Retirement	76
Resigned	76
Much Appreciated	77
Poetry	77
The Law of Nail Cutting	78
Curtain Twitching	78
A Brothers' Spat	79
Special Occasion	79
Dying to Kill	80
The Final Rage	80
Warm Thoughts	81
Rock 'n roll, baby	81
A Good Education	81
Mud Pies	82
Or	82
Like Father, like Sun	82
A Rose Arose	82
Not a clue	83
A Measure of Success	83
You don't know the half of it	83
An Owl and a Pussycat	85

Further Information

About The Author	89
By the same Author	91
Review Quotes	93

Life

Making Sense

It's not the before
it's not the after
it's not the past
or the future
it's not the above
it's not the below
it's not the yes
or the no
it's not the light
it's not the dark
the flood
or the brook
it's not the warm
or the cold
the young
or the old
it's not the outside
it's not the inside
the rock
or the sand
the rush
or the still
it's not desire
nor will
it's not the shrill
or the boom
it's not you
and it's not me,
it's the sweet and the sour
it's the seed and it's the flower
it's the first
and the last
and it's everything,
everything
in between.

Spring

I think I shall grow spring
in my garden,
open to warming rays
of returning light,
a garden that buds and bursts and blooms.
I shall not allow the dark, grey light
of weeping winter
to linger,
I'll have fresh, new light, wide-eyed dry light
firm and steady.

I shall plant my garden
not with briars and hollies, nor even roses,
but with shrubs and flowers, annuals, perennials
with roots that run and reach
and wrap, entwine and mingle,
I shall grow colour and fragrances
to revive the senses.

I think I shall grow spring
in my garden
perpetually, perfectly, protected,
shaded from scorching sun
from bright light
from fierce summer,
cooled by a temperate air,
by a whispering.

I shall not allow shaking by gusts and gales,
blustering, battering,
it shall not be shocked by sparks, flashes,
no shouts of thunder
booming above
startling strangers
nor shall I allow torrents of ripping rain,

tearing at trees,
but a soothing shy cry,
a warm tear
a quiet breeze
a hushed breath.

I think I shall grow spring
in my garden
in my wizened mind,
sprinkle soft showers
on shrivelled thought,
so that every word is compassion
every utterance, kindness,
a gentleness on every ear.

I think I shall grow spring
in my garden
every day,
every morning, afternoon, every night,
never more the endless cycle, again and again
burnt summer, a withering fall
and wasted winter,
in my spring eternal.

I think I shall grow spring,
grow spring
in the soil of my soul.

Miracles

Miracles really can happen
and sometimes when you least expect,
underground church, candlelit grotto
real inner transformation felt,
every child with their able helpers,
each year, more than fifty years,
nobody could thank enough your tireless devotion.
Cures are not sought, but friends are found,
a few days lifted above routines,
relief for loving carers,
reflection on life's cares,
old memories revived, and new ones made,
light procession
love expression.
Bent and bound by your ninety years
Even you now have your frame and chair.
Miracles really happen, in inexplicable ways

The Dry Summer

What a strange summer it had been
hardly a drop of rain from May to September.
They followed like flocks
men in shorts, young and old
some in sandals
others in white shoes
white socks clutching calves
and still others,
feet slipped into casual leather
no socks.
And women, like herds, in dresses
not those short summer frocks,
more, loosely robed to the ankles,
or in thin flowing trousers and haltered tops
like some Greek goddess.
We played in the sun
relaxed and holidayed,
there were parties, festivals,
we ate and drank together,
the first free year since the pandemic had struck.
While all around, the world darkened,
signs of war and want went unnoticed.
Then how it thundered
so sudden, so violent
louder than had those gods themselves roared
and rain so heavy the parched ground drowned,
somewhere floods destroying everything.

Then we readied for the harshest winter ever.

The coming of the Magi

2nd Jan
Christmas done
for the festive faithful,
Christmas over.
Tree down
trimmings away
fairy lights out,
no sparkle here
in New Year.
Who now sings the Twelve Days?
Has nobody heard of 'Twelfth Night'?
No hope, no bright star.
No-one around here
is waiting for wise men.

Walking a Familiar Loop

Cool sun settles on soft horizon,
clouds' caps raised above,
cold air clinging to cheeks
creeping in coats,
as we head for home
the last light moving away
in the West,
dark, bearded clouds
brush against the failing sky,
clear ground turns to hidden clumps,
footfall less sure, more stumble
slipping on soaked clay.
The last part
is always the hardest.

The Sense of an Ending

Colourless clouds
shroud the sky
sprinkling of snow
seasons the soil
shadow trees, sheltering bushes
shield the field,
no drift from ushering wind.
Watching, waiting, wondering
when to go.

Frost

Frozen night
silent white
delicate delight,
in darkness
while we slept warm in our covers
indoors,
outside
a visitation of frost
hoars sprinkled, prickly crystals
everywhere
stubbled sticks, bearded branches, spiked leaves
garland garden
spider-slung trimmings
loops of string hung plant to plant
whiskered webs, etched in air
stretched from skeins
suspended in rows,
a spiders' trapeze, a hammock
corner-strung, an ice trampoline
triangle safety net
more to catch fall, than stop flight.
concealed, hidden by day
a world of work
ice-revealed.
We awake in wonder
Not a word is heard.

Mesmerised

Two red kites
winging above
delight in flight
coiling on thermals,
look away –
and where are they?

Tenses

Today
is the first day
of the rest of my life.
The same was true
yesterday
about yesterday,
and the day before
about the day before.
I can't be so certain
about tomorrow.

No Time Like the Present

For future reference
today
is yesterday's
tomorrow.
Now,
shall we move on?

Life

Life
how fleeting
how fragile,
lived as endless,
death
always just one diagnosis
away.

Heady Days

Mrs B away
sun too fierce to be outside,
nursing a head cold
spent the day inside
by the open French windows,
a bit of reading
a bit of dozing
a bit of beering -
my kind of day.

Holiday

Holiday almost over
generous sun
soothing sea
infinity pool
and wasted days
I should have filled with more.
At first it feels it will last forever
we let days pass without care,
things tried
things to do again,
perhaps a last time
here.

Now time to pack
it's nearly time to go,
one last time for everything,
(nothing does last forever).
A journey.
A landing.
It's over.

The Price of Principle

All my life
I've been a bit of a rebel
either I'm a lone voice
resisting conformity
or I'm out of step
out of touch
out of Time.

Seeing is Believing

I have cleared the cobwebs
I have discarded the clutter
I have lit the light
I have opened my eyes.
The clouds are parting
the sun is appearing
I can feel the warmth
look up to the skies!
All that belief
all those rules
the ritual
those lies.
Now homeless
now aimless
all at sea –
how it has to be.

Sunsets

I

Mares' tails
vapour trails
fern fronds
fluffy flowers,
pulled into vertebrae
arched
combed into peaks
laid high on a pale sunset sky
a murmuration of twisting cloudlets
pink sun settles unnoticed
rests, stretched on a purple couch
whispering its shifting hues
like the changing colours of autumn,
lit underbelly, tinged cloud tops
sky failing, a fallen Rothko in blue
settles on dusty burnt sienna
a thoughtless theft from some other art.
Sun slips slowly from sight
burning a hollow in low grey clouds
copper washed on the horizon
a thousand islets floating an orange sea,
a silent protest, an afterthought palette.
Chirping swifts hover and swoop
Scooping the last light.

II

After-sun
a bar, a band
cooling copper to cobalt blue
builds and fades
strengthens again,
a disappeared sun
still a reassuring presence.
It will not last.

III

A fierce disc
crimson red
burns a crack in the clouds,
sits on a scorched horizon,
a gold bar
compressed by lead clouds,
something sets a fire
turning it molten red
flames leap from ledge,
more clouds, grey,
kindling smoke
puffing, blowing
across the fire.

IV

Oyster clouds
backwards lit,
mother of pearl edging
dazzling, glittering.

Easter

Happy Easter!
A time of rebirth
of renewal
to lift our minds
and now our hearts
to hope,
to hope
to keep faith
to think
to act
charitably.
Without Hope
what hope have we?

It's Freezing

Clocks may
go forward
an hour
this weekend,
but today
the thermometers
have gone back
a month.

Yoga Retreat

Do you stay in a yurt
eat Greek yoghourt
on a Greek yoga retreat?
From Greek yoghourt
I would retreat
From Greek yoghourt
I would run,
the reason escapes me.
Yoga, a bodily relaxation.

A Life

They say there is a first time for everything
and so there must also be a last
even if it is the first.
The way we mark out time
let each day go
never holding,
the last contact with someone
we may wish to say more
but judge best to say less
to be present
not to intrude.
The contact that says they've gone,
and you wish you'd said more
gone once more.
The last time reading a poem
listeners clearly smiling
clearly moved,
it stays in the memory.
The last time in Paris
in Rome, or was it just York?
We always meant to go back
but we went on.
Summer strolls
beer by canal
pub grub
indulging, lazing
the sun so kind to everyone.
In summer, winter is forgotten.
The last time
as if it would be forever,
we might have altered course
but we went on.

past, present, future
contained in parallel.
A life steps forth
lets go,
we grasp at the past
gasp at the future,
are held in the now.

No More to Sleep

Awake too soon
no sound
just a distant moan of a plane
going nowhere,
The street still to stir,
in the dark silence
light seeps into night,
dawn birds slightly stirring.
Impatient
waiting for the world to catch up
I sense you near.
Listening, staying still
my thoughts going nowhere.

Stained Glass

Looking through clear and coloured glass
centuries ago replaced
stained glass depictions
letting in light while losing meaning,
seeking, striving to see sky,
for something to shine into me.
Worshippers arranged in rows
queued in pews
poised in prayer
alone in private, fragmented thoughts
a congregation lost in pious reverie.
Gazing at the chancel window
almost as wide as the chancel wall,
and as tall.
A distant prelate babbling litanies,
pronouncing prayers in ritual reverence.
Is anybody listening?

Solitary Existence

Black cat
taking a toe-path walk
his private time
thinking time
time alone,
not curled up contented
satisfying human time.

Easy Life

Go easy
let me go easy,
let me go –
easy!

Flames

At Christmas, at year's end
just as new light enters
we recall lights no longer shining.
Some flames flicker and fade
and glow again,
some burn softly
lighting quietly,
a gentle warmth
for those near.
Some burn bright
catch hold
fire forests,
change the world.
The flames that burn forever in our heart
are those that never fully depart.

Hindsight

I may have been
a foolish young man
blind to foibles and follies.
Now my eyesight is getting worse,
science says it's just age
and science has ways to correct it.
They say there's no fool
like an old fool,
but science fiction comes to my aid
to give me x-ray vision.
Now, in old age nothing fools me –
I can see through everything.

Sea and Shore

As the Moon draws the sea
the sea paints the shore
rushes,
ripples of brushstrokes,
stands back
then adds some more.
Moon light
sand shadows
reveal our steps,
dry to wet,
sea teasing toes.
Footsteps of our being
washed clear,
a cleaned canvas
for other portraits.

Weather Front

It's coming
from my high window
I watch and wait
is it fog
or snow?
I don't know!

Judge Not

Don't judge;
Just enjoy.

Parting

Time up
the end of the day
we are packing away
there was nothing we could say.
We lingered lonely
barely glancing
touched without touching,
lives apart.
It's getting late
it's time to leave
solitary journeys
separate nights.
My heart is breaking,
what might have been said
those countless possibilities
now dead.
What might have been.

The Season of Goodwill is Over

That's it!
The tree's down,
trimmings down,
the crib packed away,
the Magi have 'gone home'.
We put them on a plane back to Persia,
they're not on our skilled worker list,
they'd overstayed their tourist visas.
Lord knows,
we could do with a few Wise Men.

Uninvited Guests

Tall and proud
crimsoned-crowned
scarlet-scarfed
a bunch, a group in green
a new display daily
a delight in my garden,
uninvited guests
arrived unseen,
most welcome!

Meaningful Existence

Such an exciting day,
I've hardly been able to contain myself,
this evening I've put out
the recycling bin
the green bin
and the Christmas tree.
It's the small things
that give meaning
to everything.

The Nature of Power

Some people
will say absolutely anything
to gain power.
Without power
you can say anything
but achieve
absolutely nothing.

The Sound of Silence

Listen to the silence
not voices in your head,
a coy silence,
a stop sound,
not the clamour of the everyday,
noise that captures thought
confuses clarity.
A sound
that seeps between sense and senses,
a song without words
something
between thought and feeling.
Listen!

Patter

Temperatures are rising
weather's getting wetter
it's hardly surprising
you no longer need a sweater,
a raincoat's what's required
to be appropriately attired
against rain and hail
or even a gale.
So if you think that winter's done
and even more, 'here comes the sun',
think again, think again,
there's only rain, rain
and rain!

Transformative AI

I'm sitting in the dark
it's cold
the lights are off
the TV won't come on
the washing machine hasn't started.
I've called her name clearly
carefully articulated my commands.
Maybe the wifi is down,
but Allegra isn't responding.

Seaside

Squealy gulls sky-dance
Sun sprinkles sparkles on the stretched sea
singing, skimming across wet sand.
Running ripples swim, clattering to shore
racing
each chasing
the one before.
Me, playing in the sea
dancing foot-stamps
feet splash
splash,
the cold rolls tingling my toes
creeping over feet
tumbling off ankles,
the thrill of the chill!
Me, squealing to mum
with her mobile
making, messaging pics and vids.
Me, her four-year-old kid.

Being One's Self

I'm not interested in knowing
which way the wind is blowing,
I take great pride
in swimming against the tide.
You need to know
I never go with the flow,
I've never understood
an ill wind blows no good.
If the sun's not shining
the cloud has no silver lining.

The Countryman

Coffee, cake, and quiet conversation,
there's wooden beams, an open fire and kind
friendly service, tempting treat suggestions.
The bar where pumps once stood – cakes on cake stands.

Listen! Imagine the sound of roaring
countrymen returned from fields at night,
greeting, settling scores, pushing, point-scoring.
And sense the hops and yeast with each sweet bite.

Where are they gone, those Countryman drinkers?
All level, old scores settled, all even.
Where are those jostling, boisterous workers?
Does St Peter pull the pints in Heaven?

How can I make my cake and coffee last?
I'm here this morning, drinking in the past.

Can't Afford It!

Impulsive spending.
See it. Want it. Buy it. No!
Pay for it. Remorse.

Sound Bites

Laugh at Life
walk on the sunny side
see the funny side
don't take it all as strife.

Counting

Counters
Count up
Count down
Count in
Count out
Count on,
Countdown
Counter
Discount
Count me in
Count me out
Count on me.
Discount
Viscount
Count
Countess
Countless
The Count
Head count
Counted
Countless
You count
I count
We all count
Countless count,
We. All. Count.

Love

Anniversary

Today
I have a wife
of fifty years
and she
a fifty-year-old husband.
So young!
She the patience of a saint,
I a helpless patient,
both casualties of good fortune.
Persevere
Understand
Forgive
Love.

A Couple's Couplet

If I didn't have you
I don't know what I'd do.

Gold'n

You are the cream in my coffee
You're the caramel in my toffee,
You are sticky toffee pud
You make everything taste good,
You're the honey in the hive
You make me feel alive,
You're the apple in my crumble
The support when I stumble,
You're the sweet in my dessert
You're the fruit in my [lactose free] yoghourt,
You are the apple of my eye
You're the custard on my pie,
You are strawberries and cream
Together we're a team,
You are hot chocolate sauce
On mint ice-cream, of course,
You are iced buns, cheesecake,
You're the jam in my doughnut
The jam in my scone –
Jam it, you're the one!
You're the hundreds and thousands sprinkled on my cake
You are one-in-a-million, you're no fake.
You're my ready meal
You're the real deal,
Surely, we are chalk and cheese
I cough, you sneeze,
You are roquefort, camembert, comté and brie
I may take the biscuit, but you do it for me!
You're my after-dinner chocolate
You are pure mint,
You are the tonic in my G&T –
You are definitely my cup of tea,

You are sparkling, you are still
You are warm and you are chill,
You are vintage red wine
For fifty years mine,
You, are premier Grand Cru
And I love you!

The Last Days

These are the last days
these are the best days
these are our days
these are together days
these are the days I give to you
the days you give to me.
These are free days
wasted, wanton
uncounted days,
days that are bright even when it is not
these are the days before we descend
before we go down
the days before daylight fades,
the great retreat.
These are the warmest days
these are days for living,
let us live
let us embrace
let us embrace these days
before clouds
before the dimming
before the closing of eyes
the quieting of breath.
These are those days
these are the best last days
the last best days
these are the best days
these are the last days
these are the last days…

Looking Back

Everything
I did
I did
For you.

I did
Everything
I did
For you.

For you
I did
Everything
I did.

I did
Everything
For you,
I did.

Laughter

Red or White

There is only one wine –
Red.
Everything else
is a pale imitation.

Cheers!

Wine is liquid poetry
Red or read,
more than the meaning of grapes.

Connoisseur

We all know how to drink wine –
It's taken as red.

A Poet's Life

It's not so much
ploughing your own furrow,
more
digging your own burrow.

Epitaph

A simple soul –
he did no-one any harm
and nobody
any good.

Some Hope

Every New Year
we hope
for a better year –
Every year.

Humans

A species
whose intelligence
is matched only
by its stupidity.

Touch and Go

Present card,
Approved –
Card passed (past).

No-Mow May

She walked
among fields
unmown.

Slow Down!

Oh dear
roe deer
road dead -
enough said.

No Place, Being There

Estate agents
make your business
their business.

A Word to the Wise

Pearls of wisdom
aren't always
Poetry.

Judge Not

Everyone knows
it's not the emperor's new clothes,
it's not poetry – it's prose.

My TBR List

Life is a reading competition,
so I've read,
and read,
till I'm dead.
Should have listened
to word of mouth.

The End of the Affair

Oh well
it was good while it lasted,
you bastard.

A Calling

Hired assassin —
Knife work
If you can get it.

Donkey

A donkey
is a horse
gone wonky.

Third Law of Diametrics

Action
and re-action
are equal and apposite.

Like, You Mean It

A metaphor
is something
standing for
something else.
Make sense?
A simile
is like a smile,
nearly.

Flat Earthers

As far as I can see
they'll travel as far
as the eye can see.

Ageing

I looked in the mirror
it made me think about ageing.
I decided I wouldn't.

Reflection

I am old
I am told
I tell myself –
I say it to my face.

Domestic Chores, Domestics Bores

Hang the washing up!
Hang the washing-up!
Clean clothes
dirty dishes
Hang the washing up!

Country Walk

The sign said
'Footpath and Bridal Way'.
It was a
handmaid sign.

Summer Drinks

One swallow
doesn't make
a gulp.

Summer Nights

Who would think
sleep
could be so exhausting.

De facto Descartes

I think
therefore
I can.

Opinionated Descartes

I think
therefore
I'm right.

Techie

Cometh the gadget
Cometh the man.

An Apple for Eve

God gave Moses
a new commandment
one more handed down
on a tablet –
'Thou shalt not covet
thy neighbour's technology'.

Confused

I get 'back' and 'front'
back to front.

Baldness

My hair is receding,
it needs re-seeding.

The Price of Fame/Unsung Heroes

The rich and the famous —
a plaque on all your houses!

Civic Pride

Municipal Clock —
sign of the Times.

In Mitigation

At least I haven't been as bad
as I would have been,
had I been as bad
as I could have been.

Nirvana

We're getting there,
it's painfully slow
and still some way
to go.

No Fun

There is no 'we'
in celibacy.

Sun Flour

The Sun
sets in the West
and rises
in the Yeast.

Retirement

Retirement
puts you
in a
week-end state.

Resigned

I've given up
giving up,
it's no use –
I give up.

Much Appreciated

Literary Criticism
has become
Literary Appraisal
with the emphasis very much
on praise all.

Poetry

Using words skilfully
to say things differently,
saying the familiar
in unfamiliar ways,
and always having fun
with words and meaning.

The Law of Nail Cutting

A clipping
falls to the floor
to be seen
no more.

Curtain Twitching

Have they gone away,
or just out for the day?

A Brothers' Spat

A plague
on all
your palaces!

Special Occasion

No presents, please!
(no presents please),
No! Presents, please!

Dying to Kill

Laying it on the line,
I could give my life
for the sake of others;
it's not the dying for a cause –
it's the killing.

The Final Rage

Unable to control
the fact of dying
they try to control
the act of dying

Warm Thoughts

Home
is where
the hearth is.

Rock 'n roll, baby

Shake rattle,
and roll.

A Good Education

Culture
is thicker
than nurture.

Mud Pies
Or
Like Father, like Sun

Astronomers are all
Π in the sky,
while archaeologists are really
down to earth.

A Rose Arose

Dog rose
grows
up trees –
it likes the bark.

Not a clue

Life is a puzzle
and tomorrow
is another quiz.

A Measure of Success

If the authorities
haven't come for you,
as a writer
you have failed.

You don't know the half of it

You haven't done it at all
until you've done it all.

An Owl and a Pussycat

An owl and a pussycat went to sea
They headed straight for the duty free.
There was aftershave and perfume, sweets and chocs,
Scarves and hats, and brightly coloured socks.
They filled their baskets and had both checked out
When suddenly they heard the captain shout
'Abandon ship! Abandon ship!
Don't be frightened, we're just going for a dip'.
They scrambled into lifeboats one by one,
Said Owl to the pussycat 'this will be fun'.

They splished and they sploshed, they bobbed on the brink
The boat was so heavy pussy feared it might sink,
Then up popped a pea-green fish, as plain as can be
'Don't be so frightened, it's only the sea,
If you look to your left, you'll see what I've spotted'
'A ship! A ship!' everyone shouted.
'It's sailing this way, we're going to be saved!',
So as it sailed closer everybody waved.

They climbed up rope ladders and clambered aboard
To be met by someone with a cocked hat and sword.
'Oh help! It's a pirate!' Pussycat said
'To be captured by pirates quite fills me with dread'.
'Welcome me hearties', the pirate spoke
'We'll take right good care of you gentle folk,
To feed and feast you will be our pleasure
And after we'll show you our pirates' treasure'.

They dined on mince, honey, quince, and turkey
Which they ate with a runcible spoon rather clumsily.
'And now you've enjoyed our pirates' fest
You must see what's inside our treasure chest'.

A five-pound note, plenty of money, a ring and a small guitar,
Aftershave, perfume, and more than one chocolate bar.
The pirate said 'we found it all floating, and we're looking after it,
Anyway, none of us likes smellies or chocolate,
We'll hand it all over when we return to port',
'I'll believe that when I see it', the wise Owl thought.

The sea was calm, the ship sailed fast
The harbour lights were shining – they were home at last.
Soon everyone was safely back on dry land
And they thanked the good pirates for being so kind.
Owl and Pussycat and all the passengers said
'We're going to sleep soundly when we get into bed!'

Further Information

About The Author

Chris M L Burleigh grew up in South London, and read English at Cardiff. He worked in IT. His first collection, Particles of Light, was self-published in 2017 through Troubador. His second collection, Intersecting Lines, was published by Beercott Books in 2021. He has also been a prizewinner with, and been published by, Fish Publishing. Chris is married, with three daughters, and a growing number of grandchildren.

By the same Author

Intersecting Lines: Poems
ISBN: 9781916395374 (Beercott Books, 2021)

These are poems of the everyday. Life is often serious, sometimes tragic, but it is also full of joy and playfulness. The poems celebrate life and capture the poet's response to his experience of the world, whether as a scene, a situation, or a person. Each poem paints a picture and lets the reader discover their own response.

Particles of Light: Poems, puns, word play and witty one-liners
ISBN: 9781036926281 (2nd edition, 2025)

Life is serious but is not to be lived too seriously. In this collection the familiar is shown in unfamiliar ways. Our vanity and our fragility are exposed with gentle irony, and generosity of spirit. There is something of everyone, with a section on people, places, and Nature, a short section of love poems, and a section of witty one-liners, puns, and humorous poems.

Particles of Light: Poems, puns, word play and witty one-liners Abridged for younger readers – with illustrations
ISBN: 9781707237593 (Amazon KDP, 2019)

For this abridged edition, illustrations have been added to complement many of the poems. Some poems have been removed to make this collection accessible for any younger reader ready to progress beyond poetry written specifically for children.

Review Quotes

'lyrical and beautiful…the poetry is so magical'

'the poems become something more, often resembling moving organisms, while others are more like beautifully crafted sculpture'

'a distinctive and refreshing light-hearted voice'

'An interesting voice…sensitively and nuanced, bitter-sweet, yet vibrantly playful poetry'

www.ingramcontent.com/pod-product-compliance
Lightning Source LLC
Chambersburg PA
CBHW022213090526
44584CB00013BA/836